Imani's Adventures:
Around the World I Go

Cory J. Anderson

Illustrated by Jasmine Mills

First paperback edition March 2019

Book illustrated by Jasmine Mills
Layout by W. Douglass Lyle

www.myidentityblueprint.com

Dedicated to the adventurous women in my life.
My wife Kia, daughter Nia, and mother Gloria.

I dream of going around the world exploring different places.

I dream of going around the world
to see different faces.

I dream of going around the world to explore to and fro.

I dream of going around the world,
around the world we go.

I dream of going to Asia
to walk along the Great Wall.

I dream of going to North America
to see the power of Niagara Falls.

I dream of going to Africa
and sail on the River Nile.

I dream of going to Europe
to see if the Mona Lisa smiles.

I dream of going to Antarctica
to see the penguins waddle.

I dream of going to Australia,
and maybe I will find a fossil.

I dream of going to South America to trek through the rainforest.

I dream of going to my home to tell my family about my life as a tourist.

Can you name all the Continents Imani visited?

1._____

2._____

3._____

4._____

5._____

6._____

7._____

Name all the places Imani visited

1._____

2._____

3._____

4._____

5._____

6._____

7._____

What are some places you would like to visit?

_____

_____

_____

_____

_____

_____

_____

_____

_____

_____

_____

_____

55518060R00018

Made in the USA
Middletown, DE
16 July 2019